Mindful thoughts
AT HOME

First published in the UK and North America in 2020 by

Leaping Hare Press

An imprint of The Quarto Group
The Old Brewery, 6 Blundell Street
London N7 9BH, United Kingdom
T (0)20 7700 6700
www.QuartoKnows.com

© 2020 Quarto Publishing plc

British Library Cataloguing-in-Publication Data
A catalogue record for this book is available from the British Library

ISBN: 978-0-7112-5344-5

This book was conceived, designed and produced by

Leaping Hare Press

58 West Street, Brighton BN1 2RA, UK

Publisher: *David Breuer*
Editorial Director: *Tom Kitch*
Art Director: *James Lawrence*
Commissioning Editor: *Monica Perdoni*
Project Editor: *Niamh Jones*
Design Manager: *Anna Stevens*
Illustrator: *Lehel Kovacs*

Printed in China

3 5 7 9 10 8 6 4 2

Mindful thoughts
AT HOME

Finding heart in the home

Kate Peers

Leaping Hare Press

Contents

Stay Rooted
in the Present

Mindfulness is about being truly present and fully engaged with whatever we're doing at that moment, anchoring ourselves in the present. We aim to be aware of our thoughts and feelings without getting caught up in them, letting go of distraction and judgement. We usually focus on the past or the future, but with mindfulness, we pay attention to what is around us, things that we would normally take for granted.

So why not put some focus on your home environment? The layout, ambience and décor in your home can offer a perfect complement to the sense of wellness that mindfulness creates. It is our home, after all.

What does 'home' mean, really? While your home is a statement to all who visit, more importantly, it influences your mood and emotions. The vision of a beautiful house means something different to everyone, so it is important to be confident with your choices and content in what you have around you.

Often, we forget about what is really important in life, striving for perfection in an imperfect world. Mindfulness can help to right that wrong. In our homes, we have some amount of control over our surroundings and can decide what makes us truly happy – there is no need to follow a trend, decorate, or create a home set-up that doesn't please you. If we look at the things that we own, decide what we need and make sure we have the key ingredients for a soothing base for our lives, then we can make a space that allows us to feel safe, be calm and create memories.

It actually doesn't take much to give a space a radical makeover. A coat of paint or some upcycled furniture can make a huge difference, helping turn a room from a depressing environment to a place where you feel positive and productive. If this sounds a bit abstract, let's take an example: consider the humble rug. The right choice grounds a space, adding warmth and acting as a focal point from which you can build. Rather than going for whatever someone tells you is 'in' right now, or grabbing something in a hurry because 'it'll do', you can bring in some mindfulness: consider how the fabric will feel against your bare feet. Likewise, rearranging furniture needn't just be about dragging things around; it can help you evaluate your space and think over what you really need from it.

If your space is making you unhappy, focus and reflect on what you love in your room and build your scheme around that. Making small, deliberate changes will help you feel content in your environment, and with mindful awareness you can become more alert to how to please as many of your senses as possible. This book aims to show you ways to manage your home into a delightful and comfortable environment.

What Turns a **House** into a **Home?**

A house offers protection from the elements, but for it to be a home, there must also be an emotional pull. Our homes should be places where we can retreat from the world and feel relaxed. Choosing a house or apartment is a practical business, dictated by requirements such as location, cost and size, and it always comes down to circumstances, finances and, where possible, our gut reaction when we walk through the door. But while a house or apartment is four walls, a home is our sanctuary, an environment that gives us a special feeling. With care, we can make any house our home.

A HOME THAT MAKES YOU HAPPY

When thinking of the kind of place that makes feel good, it is important to know why. Are our happy places full of colour, or soothingly neutral? Are they peaceful, or resonant with friends chatting and music playing? We are constantly told we need the next new thing for our lives, but the feeling of our home cannot be bought; it comes from the relationship we have with it. To make that real, we need a good understand of what we really feel.

The property you live in might not be your ideal, and very few of us live somewhere that an interiors magazine would be eager to photograph, but that doesn't mean we can't make a home that feels right and reflects who we are. Rarely do people find a home with no compromise – perhaps the neighbours play loud music or the closest shop is a ten-minute drive. Whether you live in a shared flat or luxury mansion, it won't be your own unless you are aware of your emotional response to your surroundings.

CREATING OUR UNIQUE ENVIRONMENT

Houses do not need to be perfect, but we can adjust those things within our control. Mindfulness means being present in every moment. Just take a look around your space now; don't try to force any reactions, but see how you feel. What do you appreciate? Maybe the smooth, green leaves on a house plant or the comfort of a pillow get your shoulders unknotting. Maybe there's washing-up in the sink; is it bothering you enough to prioritise, or does it feel more important to finish a conversation and spend time with loved ones? Just sit with your feelings a moment; there's no right answer.

You can also get a sense of balance if you approach bigger decisions mindfully. For instance: are you contemplating changes? A new sofa or better lighting are aesthetically pleasing and can give us a mindful space, but if they put us into debt or clutter our rooms then what we have already can be enough. Again, take a moment to sit peacefully with your feelings. If you're frustrated that right now it's more sensible to keep a tatty old couch, for instance, just let that frustration flow through you. Don't fight it – it won't hurt you. Sit with it mindfully, and it will pass.

Of course, a home isn't just the objects within it; it's also what you do there. Friends in the kitchen, sharing a meal, laughter and shared memories; a shower after a long walk or a bath with a book: all these create moments to be present in. There is no right or wrong answer when considering what makes your home right for you, perhaps a well-stocked fridge, a comfy bed and movie night every Sunday. The smell of cooking wafting through the kitchen, warmth in the winter, being safe and secure – what makes you feel content?

A home should provide you with a safe haven, a place where your emotional needs can be met and you can be yourself. Things can get overlooked when creating your space – elements that not only create a sanctuary for you, but are also easy, free, and within your reach. Laughter costs nothing; sleep costs nothing; relaxation is within everyone's budget. As time passes we will enter different stages of our lives, a family may grow and the way we use our space will change – just as we develop, so do our homes around us. People can get into a routine about sleeping on their side of the bed or sitting in a certain spot on the sofa but it can be good to shake it up. Rearranging and redecorating a home can bring about positive change. All that really matters is that it reflects us, our lives and our personalities; if we can do this, the rest will fall into place.

Making Time
for
Solitude

There is no need to head for the hills and live in a monastery to bring spirituality into the home; we can create spaces in which to sit, contemplate, meditate and

breathe wherever we are. If we can find some calm in the home, it allows us to head out into the world recharged and rested, ready to face whatever the day brings. Whether we're in a large, loud family or a small city-centre apartment, there is always a way to create a spiritual space that works for you.

FINDING CALM

For some, the biggest hurdle to spiritual growth at home is their conviction that, to grow spiritually, they need to live a minimalist Zen life with no possessions. This attitude prevents many from even trying to incorporate simple practices into daily life. The truth is, people are always people and bare surroundings aren't magic: ancient Buddhist writings illustrate how, despite having few possessions and a life focusing solely on spirituality, even monasteries were not free from personal tensions, disagreements and jealousies.

Society has changed beyond comparison since these early fifth-century texts. Today, life in the home offers more freedom and opportunities for new activities, perhaps learning a language, writing a book, setting up a new business, doing a live online yoga class – all in the comfort of our own front rooms. So given all the busyness of modern life, how do we make space for our souls?

CREATE A SPIRITUAL SPACE

Create a space where the busyness stops. As author and activist Anne Lamott says, 'Almost everything will work again if you unplug it for a few minutes, including you'. There are various ways to do this, and you don't need to set aside a whole room. You might set up a reading nook, or putting a chair by a window to sit down to reflect and look out. Some people love to create a sacred area, and use flower petals and often a statue or icon of worship. You can even make a tiny sacred space just in your own field of vision: gazing at a candle flame is a great focal point when relaxing and slowing down. Owning this space in the home helps to take you out of the daily life and ground you into a more spiritual practice. You can create very simple rituals, such as listening to a meditation app when you have a spare moment, or writing a gratitude journal first thing in the morning to get the day off to a positive start, or just sit quietly and let the world wash over you.

What about living with children and other people? Does this make it more of a challenge for us to create a mindful, peaceful space in the home? In some ways, yes: there's no point pretending that children are always creatures of quiet contemplation and perfect stillness. As well as being enchanting, they are noisy and demanding, calling for our emotional energy, our practical care and our constant attention. Bringing up children can be all-encompassing, but at the same time teach us many lessons about ourselves, cultivating skills in patience, endurance and generosity. Living with others takes away privacy, but can also offer companionship and, hopefully, emotional support (even if it also sometimes calls on us to be patient as well). It may be difficult to find a silent moment, but even if you can only manage a few minutes in a corner while the racket goes on nearby, or have to wait till the kids are asleep, you can try putting on some headphones, closing your eyes, and creating a quiet space within yourself. All this is excellent discipline, but it's also quite all right to ask others to give you time to reset. There's nothing selfish about making sure you're well and happy enough to be your best self around those you love.

Harnessing **Energy** in the **Home**

The feeling that you get when you open the front door can affect the next few hours inside your home. The doorway is known as the 'mouth of chi', the threshold between the outside world and your private space. It's a good idea to keep this area neat and uncluttered, so that we can breathe freely and enjoy our space.

Being mindful of our surroundings, we are more likely to feel positive when approaching our front door if it is clear, clean and welcoming, so when you have the time, get rid of any overgrown plants or rubbish bins blocking the pathway. Clean the windows, wipe down the front door, perhaps even freshen up the paintwork if it's peeling or the colours are dull. Once inside, pay attention to the entrance area – a place to hang your coat and bag may not be enough. Stand in this space a moment and consider what you could add or remove to help free up space. You need somewhere for coats, shoes, post bags and possibly keys; could it be better organized? Do some setting up, sweep and clean, and make it as bright and welcoming as possible.

Opening the front door will be a completely different experience the next time you arrive home, and this can create a positive link with your space from the moment you step inside. Creating an organized space in this area allows the process of entering and leaving to be smooth, while inviting beneficial energy to make its way throughout the rooms and the rest of the house.

HELP POSITIVE ENERGY TO FLOW

Consider adding elements of Yin and Yang within your home. What does that mean, you may wonder? Put simply, the Yin-Yang theory states that the universe is composed of two opposite, complementary and deeply intertwined forces: Yin (passive and receptive) and Yang (active and energetic). By introducing this concept into our homes and achieving the balance that is right for us, we can harness their energy to support our own mindful practice.

The two types of energy make sense alongside each other when you understand what each one means. In essence, there are places in the house where you'll want to be lively and get things done, and places where you'll want to chill out; it's just a matter of matching the energy of the room to its purpose. For instance: places where you'll want to relax, such as a bathroom, thrive best when they have Yin energy, with softer shades and tranquil colours. On the other hand, you'll want to be efficient and alert when you're busy in your work space, so strong colours, bright lights and a feeling of lively Yang is what you'll want to invigorate you there.

CREATING THE RIGHT SORT OF ENERGY

The goal of feng shui is to create a space that sustains and supports us, keeping opposites in balance to promote the energy we need. In a working area such as the kitchen, we need a clear area for the food we are preparing, so we can get a sense of the colours and textures of the ingredients as we put together a meal, stimulating our appetite and being mindful of our actions as we peel, chop and stir. In the bedroom, we need soft lights to promote relaxation, clearing away all the thoughts that are crowding our minds after the events of the day, preparing us for a restful sleep.

By following feng shui principles, we are ultimately creating a home where our surroundings reflect and influence our inner selves, serving as a constant reminder of what is meaningful and important in the way we live. It's not a complicated science: it's just a question of understanding ourselves and our needs, and shaping our environment to support them. We are mindful of our path in life and how we connect to things around us every moment, day and night. When we do this, we are being truly present in our spaces.

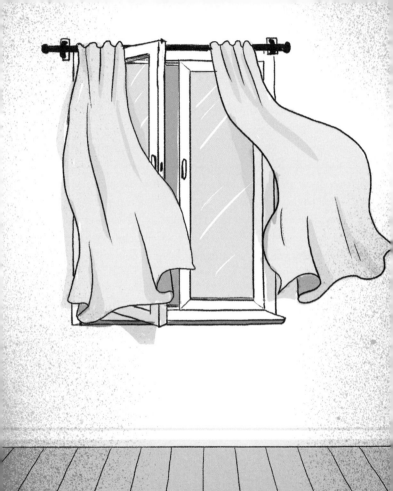

Spiritual
Upkeep of the
Home

We all want to feel at ease in our living space, but it's often easier said than done. When we have jobs, hobbies and social lives, it's easy to let our houses turn into mere holding areas for our stuff, but if we perform some spiritual upkeep, we can prevent the energy getting stuck. Even if you don't spend lots of time at home, it still functions as your base, and if you view it in this light, you may feel able to care for it in the same way you care for yourself.

HARMONY AND CALM

We all want our homes to be safe havens, but the reality is that sometimes, upsetting things happen, and memories and emotions can linger behind. If that starts to block your contentment, it may be time to clear the way for some positive energy to flow.

Different civilizations throughout time have used spiritual home cleansing rituals to clear negative energy. Native Americans chased away bad spirits with the use of drums and rattles; medieval Europeans used salt along with prayer for the same purpose; myrrh and frankincense were used to bring blessings to homes in the Middle East; and harmony was brought into Chinese homes with the use of chanting, incense, and gongs. If any of those ideas appeal to you, it's fine to try them out, but if you want something closer to your own culture, you don't necessarily need to use those specific practices. It does make sense, though, to try a few daily rituals to help you feel more at peace within your own home.

SWEEP WORRIES ASIDE

During the day, open up the windows, pull up the blinds and curtains, plump up the cushions, sweep the floor, dust down the surfaces. While you don't need to spend unnecessary time creating an immaculate environment, keeping your home pleasing to the eye will make it a more restful space to spend time in. In darker areas, lamps that emit natural-looking light can change how a space feels. Essential oils in a diffuser can help with unwanted smells coming in from the outside, such as a neighbour's cooking or polluted air. If air quality is an issue where you live, consider investing in an air purifier or house plants.

Incense has been used for centuries to drive away negative energies and calm and soothe the mind. In Buddhism, it is more than just an offering: it is believed to benefit the mind, and several scientific studies support this. The smell of incense in the home can be very healing, helping to calm nervous tension and clear the air after arguments. It is also great as a barrier between you and any disruptive neighbours. Simply burn the incense, allow the smoke to disperse throughout and walk around your home, announcing clearly that your aim is to fill the space with love and positivity.

CREATING POSITIVE FEELINGS

If you have housemates, try doing them small kindnesses without expecting anything in return. Perhaps do the washing-up when it's not your turn, cook a special meal or buy some colourful flowers to brighten up your shared space. Of course, not all housemates are perfect when it comes to doing their share, so make sure that you're not doing this to make them feel guilty, or, more subtly, to set them an example you want them to follow. Point-scoring when it comes to jobs does nothing for either party. Instead, do it just to be nice, to show that you're willing to do things to make everyone comfortable. The simple act of being generous without being asked creates a good feeling for you and those you live with, encouraging a better atmosphere in your home.

When the hectic pace of modern life sends your energy in the wrong direction, pull out a yoga mat. Whether you are feeling the foundations through your toes, breathing in the soothing scents of your home environment, or stretching up high and sending out your good intentions and awareness into the building, getting back into your body can make you feel more grounded and present.

Cleaning is Good for You

The sight of a basin piled high with washing-up can make your heart sink. The clothes make it from the wash basket into the machine promptly after wearing them, only to be sitting clean on the floor for days before they are folded, ironed and put away. Cleaning is rarely something that people describe as a fulfilling activity; rather, we enjoy having done it once it's finished. Our own internal chatter and guilt when faced with the relentlessness of cleaning our homes can drag us down.

FINDING THE POSITIVES

There are mindful ways in which we can approach this. If we feel down when looking at the dirt or mess in our homes, for instance, we could acknowledge this and consider the action of cleaning as one of self-care rather than a boring obligation. The action of cleaning can be beneficial in many ways; it is an opportunity to observe our feelings and thoughts, becoming a regular meditation in the home. So, the practice of cleaning is not only good for your environment, but also good for the mind. It is not uncommon for therapists to recommend cleaning the home to help patients suffering from depression. Cleaning gets you moving, boosting the endorphins.

Once we make the decision to clean, we can become interested in the physical sensations we experience. How does the water feel on our hands? What do the smells of the products evoke in our minds? Natural cleaning products using lemon and bicarbonate of soda (baking soda) will freshen our home, and the scent of lemon is well known for uplifting your mood, providing a boost of energy and promoting mental clarity and focus – a bonus you can feel straight away. Notice a sense of being grounded through your feet as you stand at the sink; notice the water temperature, the smell of the washing-up liquid. Feel the sensations of the bubbles and movement on your hands as you are washing plates. Be grateful for having hot water to wash the dishes, something that we often take for granted.

Mindfully freeing ourselves from our own judgements means that it is okay to find cleaning monotonous at times. That's all right: boredom is an authentic emotion just like any other, and you're allowed to feel it. Don't punish yourself for not feeling the 'right' way about cleaning; just feel what you feel. Make friends with your boredom. You might find yourself doing a better job; if you can find meaning in something as mundane as cleaning, then you've got the foundation for a very fertile life

WORKING TOGETHER

Sometimes being mindful means asking people that you live with to do more chores in the home: trying to become a more mindful cleaner doesn't mean you have to be the only one doing it. When others take their turn, it gives you an opportunity to practise appreciation, and occasionally they need a nudge to get involved. Don't worry – this is all part of the process. Whether it's picking up a pair of socks from the bathroom floor or washing up a breakfast bowl, cleaning should feel like something that every house member can be involved in, and there's nothing wrong with asking for assistance. If you work as a team, the process will be quicker, and may even present opportunities for fun and reflection together.

There are two aspects to cleaning, the actual spraying and wiping, and the tidying things away to keep the area clear. Both aspects boost your state of mind by removing clutter, freeing up headspace to focus on preferred activities, such as meditation, enjoying meals with friends or reading a book. There is no endgame with cleaning. Yes, we can clean and dry the dishes and put them away, and yes, as we are doing this, dust is settling elsewhere in the house that needs cleaning too. This is similar to meditation practice: as we observe our anxieties about the apparently endless cleaning, perhaps we can let go of some of the less essential tasks, and clean what we can with a spring in our step. If you wake up and feel unable to wash the dishes, this is okay, drop the guilt, return to it later when you feel more energized. This is all a process.

Accepting Change

Things go wrong in all aspects of life, including in the home. The washing machine breaks just when you need an outfit for job interview the next day. A leak comes through the ceiling from the flat above, damaging a treasured possession. The front door lock stops working with the key inside, leaving us unable to get in or out when we are in a rush to be somewhere. We do not choose for any of these things to happen; they are out of our control and the only thing we can possibly have power over is our response to them.

Of course none of this is good news, but there is a silver lining: it's a chance to hone your patience. The more you train your mind to meditate in the predictable and comfortable environment of your home, the easier it will be to practice mindfulness when you find yourself facing difficult circumstances in less familiar surroundings.

DEALING WITH CURVEBALLS

When life knocks us for six, there is often a tendency for the mind to resist what is happening. This simply creates more suffering, because the problem is not going away. Our bodies go into fight or flight patterns, releasing the hormone cortisol (which is quite bad for them if it doesn't get a chance to dissipate); our brains become anxious; we feel pretty sorry for ourselves. Why should this happen to us, we ask?

However, once the initial reaction has passed, it's time to move on. When facing a possible disaster, the first step in mindfulness is to observe your thoughts. Bring yourself into the present by being aware of your thoughts, allowing them to happen, but separating them from your reaction to them.

AND BREATHE

Even during a situation that requires you to act, you need to take breaks to operate well, otherwise your mind will burn out and you'll freeze yourself at a time when you need to take decisive action.

When we are under immense stress, it can be easy to forget to take a break. We are in high adrenaline mode, constantly trying to do something; we want to solve the situation instantly, and it can feel like there is no time to think. Making time to sit and meditate during periods of stress, putting things into perspective and reminding ourselves of what we do have to be grateful for can help greatly.

Stop to notice the coolness of the air as you breathe in through your nose and the warmth your body gives that air as you breathe out through your mouth. See if you can be kind to yourself as you breathe, let go of any judgements and self-pity you may have, or acknowledge them and allow them to drift by. Set an intention for your meditation as you sit and fill in the blanks; 'I am calm and content.' Remember that if good intentions and calm don't arise straight away, they will come in their own time. There is no need to force anything or get impatient.

USING A MANTRA

There can be a mantra at this stage that this too shall pass. It is a temporary problem. There is an old Persian fable that the phrase most universally true, no matter what the situation, is: 'This too shall pass.' When it comes to dealing with domestic frustrations, there are few mantras more applicable. Whatever you're coping with, it will eventually, like all things, pass away. We know that perhaps the washing machine will cost us money to fix; it could even get us into debt because we will have to borrow the money before we are able to get it mended. Stop. Before you build catastrophe on catastrophe, take a deep breath. We have the power to act and seek solutions in future, and we don't have to panic just because we haven't yet reached them. We can

44

get by without it for a while, and we can feel gratitude once the crisis has passed.

Using a mantra in times of crisis can ground us, allow us to take a few deep breaths, and override the negative thoughts that are crowding into our minds. A mantra can help us observe the actual severity of the situation as opposed to the initial reaction, and help us see the end in sight. The inevitable ups and downs of life are going to occur whether we want them to or not, but we can learn how to maintain calm emotions through our mindful practice each day.

The Benefits of
Unfinished
Projects

Whether we have lived in one home or several, it is the special memories that stay with us. For me that means decorating the Christmas tree, seeing my toddler taking his first steps in the kitchen, toasting marshmallows, my tiny one-bed flat with my boyfriend – it was noisy and had ugly yellow carpets, but it was ours, and somewhat exciting. I am grateful for a roof over our heads, for warmth, for the fact that I had the opportunity to live in several homes.

Whether you love your home or not, you can choose to be thankful for it. There are times when it's not so easy to be grateful for what we have: we simply see the negative, and once we have seen it, it can be hard to train ourselves to see the positive. We look at the projects we haven't completed – the painting that needs finishing, the book we picked up to try something new but haven't got further than the first page. We should be doing better. Why haven't we got everything under control? Surely we are failing and everyone else has their house in order?

FOCUS ON WHAT MATTERS

Comparisons can be difficult to avoid. We visit friends in their new home: the garden is bigger than ours, they recently fitted a new kitchen and finished the entire project on time; they have nicer soft furnishings, more space. A feeling of missing out takes over, we begin comparing our home to theirs, wishing for the things that appear to be lacking in our own home; perhaps they are, but by comparing we are putting focus on the wrong place. We can only control our own life, and we should avoid wasting our time and energy focusing on what we perceive other people are achieving that we are not. Comparisons do not add any contentment to our lives. On the contrary, they can make us feel bitter towards others and detract from our happiness. Some of the best things in life are hidden from sight: love, kindness and empathy are rarely measured, and when we take a look at the importance of these qualities versus material things, it can remind us to be present, to be kind to not only ourselves but also our surroundings. Comparing our unfinished projects to how we see other homes can damage to our self-esteem. Things are not always as they seem and just because someone may have finished their kitchen project, they may be having difficulties in other areas of their life where you are thriving. And even if they don't, that doesn't harm you or take away from what you have. View them with the same generosity you'd hope they feel towards you.

TRY A HOME MISSION STATEMENT

Remind yourself of your own worth, quiet your inner critic, and embrace self-compassion. By doing these things you can try to slow down the negative thoughts about your surroundings. Look at the priorities in your life, the things that are non-negotiable to you for your day-to-day wellbeing and happiness. Create yourself a home mission statement and suddenly, you will find decision-making with regards to your house very simple.

For example, if your home mission statement is to be open and welcoming to loved ones, then creating a good seating area in the kitchen for mealtimes is an easy decision to make. This may not be the time to renovate your kitchen, but going through the cupboards that you started decluttering a few months ago but never finished is an opportunity to give your no-longer-needed pots and pans to others in need, while completing a project at the same time. The stacks of papers on the kitchen side waiting to be sorted and organized are opportunities for you to feel growth and accomplishment, and the piles of stuff to sift through on the dining-room table are opportunities to make the space more comfortable so you can reconnect with friends and family over a homemade dinner.

Instead of letting an unfinished project get you down or make you feel stressed, just remember that all you need to do is make time to start again and then it will be finished; just think how satisfying that will be. We can work hard to learn the difference between learning from others and unhealthy competitiveness. Notice which attitudes prompt positive change at home and which result in negative feelings. Our homes belong to us; we can choose how we feel while we are in them and our mission statement will help focus on this.

The World
on Your Plate

People often congregate in the kitchen. It can be the busiest room in the home, the location for a whole range of domestic activities, and also a social hub. If a visitor stops by, it's the kitchen we go to for a cup of tea. If we have a table in there, this provides a warm and inviting place for the children to do their homework while the enticing aromas of the evening meal fill the room.

Whether we're lucky enough to have a big cosy kitchen or not, it is never just to store and prepare the food. We work in there to create the meals that celebrate the company of friends and family, where spontaneous kitchen discos can happen as we feel free to dance to the radio, a chance to let go and have some silliness in our lives.

A MINDFUL KITCHEN

The kitchen offers one of the best places in the home to practise mindfulness. We can take time to observe exactly what we are putting into our bodies, and remind ourselves of the benefits food can bring to our minds. How we feel when we finish a meal can shape the next few hours, our moods and our actions. A sugary takeaway may provide a quick fix, but the post-mealtime slump can make us feel lethargic and head for the TV controller rather than choosing a different activity; there's no need to be too purist about food, but dinners prepared at home do us good when we can manage them.

There is an ancient belief that the cook imbues a meal with a light touch of their own emotions. Preparing our own food is an act of self-care, we are nourishing our bodies and minds and this helps us physically and mentally, reminding us to look after ourselves the best we can.

Many mindfulness practices take place in yoga studios or meditation spaces where the surroundings are peaceful. The real meditation starts to take place when it's intimately integrated into daily life. Whenever you notice that you lose presence and start thinking about something from the past or future rather than being here and now, stop what you are doing, take five deep breaths and observe what you are creating. Continue with the activity and try to remain present; before long it will become more natural and effortless. Your cooking will be more inspired, you will be more nourished by the food you are creating and more aware of its flavours and taste.

We all remember a certain dish from our childhood, the emotion and the nostalgic feeling it generates comes from how the food was prepared. The next time you are in the kitchen, chop slowly, smile and cook with love.

SLOW IT DOWN

Having a functional and modern kitchen is truly a blessing. It helps turn meal preparation into a pleasurable activity amidst the busy hustle and bustle of life. How often are we mindful of this space and the activities that take place within it?

We often race around the kitchen, grabbing things out of the cupboards, perhaps with people chatting around us, without paying much attention to the process of cooking and the energy going into it. When we do this, we missing that opportunity to be mindful and slow down. Kids come running in needing help with homework; the phone rings; the doorbell chimes. Rather than getting flustered, it helps to see these interruptions as a chance to interact with others, a natural rhythm between one mindful way and another. We can then return to the process of meal preparation, settling back into a quieter focus. Peeling and chopping vegetables can be a gentle, meditative process; notice the colours and textures of the food you handle, being mindful about using all parts of the vegetables and reducing waste. Take in the smells whilst chopping, notice whether you are rushing to get the jobs done, and perhaps try to pace yourself and see if this makes a difference. And if you can't cook from scratch every day, don't be hard on yourself: even throwing convenience foods into the microwave is feeding the body and, if you do it with kindness and attention, the spirit.

Folding with
Love

Clothes are often seen as a way of expressing our personalities. When we are young, we are often bound by school uniform restrictions, or wear the clothes that our parents have chosen for us, but in adulthood we can make our own decisions. How lucky we are to have the clothing selections online and in stores, thrift shops and online sales channels: we can we can get the things we love for less and, when buying second-hand, avoid the environmental impact of producing more new clothes.

Despite our fondness for finery, though, the sight of an overflowing washing basket can make us groan. Can reminding ourselves to be grateful for what we have change the way we do our laundry?

RESPECT YOUR CLOTHES

The downside to this vast choice is a fast-fashion culture that has filled our wardrobes to the brim; we can wear a different item every day without having to wash our clothes for a week or two, until one day there are no clean socks and the underwear drawer is empty. Instead of chucking each item into the laundry bin, perhaps we can be a little more mindful of our actions at the end of the day and try to avoid washing our clothes unnecessarily.

The constant washing and drying of clothes reduces their lifespan and is bad for the environment. When undressing at night, we can take a look at for any marks on otherwise clean clothes. If possible, dab clean with a wet cloth, so the item can be worn again. Calmly examining each item for holes or dirt makes us appreciate what we have and brings us into the moment; our minds are focused on something simple.

Do you sort your clothes to keep light and darks separate, keeping them at their best for longer, or is everything thrown in together, without giving it a second thought? Here is an opportunity to observe the speed at which you operate in the home; if you are completely present when getting undressed, these laundry decisions can be made with each item, every day.

TAKING CARE OF WHAT WE HAVE

There are times when I have tried to put on an item of clothing from my wardrobe only to find out that it shrank in the wash – which was entirely my own fault. I may have been getting changed one evening, then thrown my dress across the room into the laundry basket with the rest of my clothes without thinking about the fact that it needed to be washed at a low temperature. We lead busy lives, and most people have a corner of the room where they pile garments at the end of the day, but being more mindful in our homes means trying to make time to take care of all of our belongings, clothes included.

When doing laundry for others, we are folding with love. A parent might enjoy the clean, fresh smell as they put away the laundered clothes, ready for their child to wear. The act itself makes us feel nurturing; we are taking care of others. We can bring this care and loving attention to our own clothing too: our softest sweatshirts are often the ones we have washed countless times, making them cosy, protecting us from the elements and keeping us warm indoors. Some of our clothes might bring back special memories, we might associate them with happy times; we can reflect on this while we are storing them away, ready to wear next time.

Remind yourself how lucky you are to have these clothes. One reason we update our wardrobe is to feel in control: it's good for your confidence to present yourself to the world in a positive way. But that's not the only way to take control; you can also exercise thought, skill and mastery in how you maintain what you have, making everything last as long as possible and treating it with care. Think about your belongings;

do you really need more? Can you mend a little hole appearing in a jumper to avoid it from spreading further? We don't need many things to wear; think about rotating the various outfits rather than buying more to add to your wardrobe. This act of mindfulness can bring you straight into the present when doing the laundry, and as we dress ourselves every day, it will help us feel gratitude for the abundance we already possess.

Open Doors to
Open Our Hearts

How would you feel if there were a knock on the door and a friend turned up unexpectedly? Would the idea of someone seeing your house untidy and well lived-in make you feel inadequate? In earlier eras, it was less of an issue for people drop in for a quick hello, but nowadays, the idea of unannounced visitors brings many of us out in a cold sweat. We worry about the mess. This need not be the case; we should remind ourselves that having a perfectly tidy and clean home is not a reflection of our worth as human beings. The home is a space for connection, and we can begin to connect by looking at those we are closest to and inviting people in.

THE HOME AS A SOCIAL SPACE

The journey of mindfulness is about thinking what is important to you, choosing what you want to keep in life. For most people, seeing friends and family is high up on their list of what makes them feel good. With our busy lives and the rise of digital communication such as texting, video calls and email, we often physically see people less than we would like to – including talking face-to-face with those we live with. We can change this and make ourselves more comfortable with inviting people over even when the house is in a mess, simply to share some food and catch up; it's time to let go of the need to have our house looking like a show home or having a gourmet meal on offer. Likewise, we can make more of an effort with those we are living with. When we communicate more with them, it will remind us to stay in touch with our wider circle. Nobody else's home is perfect either, and if you can invite guests into a warm, friendly disorder, they'll probably be glad to come.

INVITE FRIENDS IN

Start slowly by making new connections; try something you haven't done in a while, like inviting a neighbour round or dropping in on a friend that you haven't seen recently (assuming you can be fairly confident they'll be glad to welcome you). This will allow them to do the same for you, and reminds us how good it feels to be around people. By visiting others, we will see that their lives are not perfect either, and this reduces anxiety if people come to our own homes.

Our homes give us the opportunity to learn how to be more tolerant, and teach us how to open up to new experiences. Keeping people out can make us feel lonely; inviting them in brings a chance to share laughter and joy.

Some have been asked on their deathbeds what has meant the most to them during their lives, and the most common answer is relationships, friends and shared moments. We are at risk of becoming increasingly disconnected from those immediately around us with the uptake in the use of social media. Humans crave physical companionship with other humans; we need it to stave off depression and loneliness. By all means use social media to connect with loved ones far away, but for those within travelling distance, don't let it crowd out actual time together. Use it to arrange visits instead; make things real.

MAKE TIME FOR OTHERS

In the home, we can slip into habits without realising. As a parent, for instance, you might turn down the offer of a family movie to get on with jobs around the home; as a result your family might stop asking you to join them, even if you change your mind. We all have lots to do, but don't forget to remain accessible – or, if you're developing the reputation of 'the person too busy to talk and play', take some time to reach out.

We can aim to be truly present when spending time with those that we love. Stop the multi-tasking when friends come to visit; once the tea is made, leave the washing-up until the conversation is finished or your guest has gone. Sit and slow down with those around you. An essential ingredient of a mindful life is time. One of the most impactful things you can do to help yourself live more mindfully is to make time and space for the things you really value; connections with others are often at the heart of what makes people genuinely happy.

The
Bathroom

One of the best rituals to end a frantic day is a hot bath – although if you're more of a shower person, the rush and tingle of hot water that offers can be just as good.

Even the simple daily ritual of washing our faces each morning and evening, touching our skin, brings us into our bodies and performs an act of self-care.

A THERAPEUTIC RITUAL

Baths have been such a huge part of human health that every continent has its own bathing tradition. In ancient times, herbal baths were used to help the sick, while mineral baths were considered effective for detoxification. Some cultures even believed that bathing offered good luck and protection. Romans built huge complexes with under-floor heating, Scandinavians plunge in cold water after a sauna and the Japanese have developed the art of bathing in a smaller, specially designed 'soaking bath tub' that allows you to sit up while being deeply submerged. These are designed primarily to relax a tired body and give you time to collect your thoughts and inspirations. They are designed not for hygiene, but for peaceful meditation and calm: in some cultures, people even give themselves a quick wash before getting into the tub, having a completely clean soak. Even if we only take a deep bath every month, the experience gives our minds some time to slow down.

CONNECTING WITH OURSELVES

Bathing allows us to bring full awareness to our body, checking in with every part of ourselves both physically and mentally. Washing gives us an opportunity to take care of our physical vessels, to clean away any dirt and bacteria along with our troubles and anxieties. Bring awareness to each part of your body as you wash; practise being thankful for the wondrous vehicle that you inhabit, and grateful that you have a calm space to use for just this purpose.

The actions of washing and drying ourselves can be a grounding ritual that offer an opportunity to settle our flighty minds, which might still be racing after a day of constant use.

There is something about washing that cleanses the mind as well as the body. Our muscles have their own knowledge: each time we wash our hands we perform several actions without thinking about them. Observing these rituals allows us to become present in the moment. We roll up our sleeves, put the plug into the sink and fill it up. We reach for the soap and we can look at the sensations we feel, combining water with lather and massaging our hands, adding a little pressure to the parts that may need it. Notice the texture of the towel against your hands; how does it feel? And how good is it once our hands are clean?

A PEACEFUL SPACE

A mindful bathroom can be created with nature in mind, using greenery to incorporate the outdoors within your four walls, as well as oxygenating the air. A good bathroom is efficient, of course, but it can also be set up for enjoyment, a meditative space for rest and rejuvenation. For those wondering how best to create a verdant space, air plants, bamboo and succulents are commonly used in bathrooms to withstand the steam from hot showers and water. Work with the nature of the plants, and they'll reward you.

Half an hour in a bath with some peace and quiet allows us to slow down to an absolute stop, allowing ourselves to have space to think, to not think, or simply be present with our calming surroundings. Parents can relish the solitude of the bathroom once children are asleep, the soothing noises calming the senses after a hectic day. It's like pushing the reset button, whether you have a shower to wake up or a bath to relax and create calm. We emerge as a new and fresher version of ourselves.

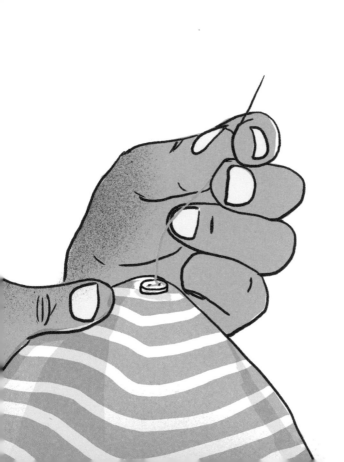

Restore,
Repair & Fix

Gone are the days when we would typically fix something rather than throwing it out; we have become a throwaway society. It can be easy to call a professional when something breaks or buy a replacement, but often you could mend it yourself and save the money. If we don't try, then we will never learn new skills such as repairing holes in the walls or fixing the kitchen cabinet, or feel the satisfaction gained when we take control of our own surroundings.

MAKE DO AND MEND

The idea of learning a new skill to repair a leaky tap or a broken chair leg increases your self-reliance, making you less likely to panic when things go wrong. It's a great feeling to look around your home and feel that you've maintained it yourself. And whether it's fixing a radio or painting a piece of furniture, the process of repair can be turned into a mindful exercise. The process allows us to concentrate calmly on an absorbing challenge, and when it's completed successfully, it boosts our self-esteem and gives us the satisfaction of looking at the fruits of our labour. (Or, if the repair really doesn't work, it at least gives us the chance to learn new skills and practice mindfully dealing with frustration.) By repairing our home and possessions, we are also maintaining ourselves.

Our grandparents would probably have had the skills to mend most household items, and things were commonly passed down through families and repaired on the way. Modern goods are mass-produced, and we can replace them cheaply, rather than bothering to fix them. We are piling up landfills with things that could be reused, whereas buying new means more transportation, storage costs and packaging, using natural resources and increasing global emissions.

Social events are taking place where the public can bring along broken electrical items and attempt to repair them with some support. The aim is simply to extend the lifetime of electrical equipment and reduce the amount that becomes waste.

One word of caution before we go on. Many repairs at home can be done with little experience – but do ensure you research anything that you don't understand, particularly if you are dealing with electricity. Likewise, an important part of mindfulness is to be aware of our own faults, and often this can be taking on too much ourselves. Calling in help from friends or professionals can be a good thing; we need to step back and think about when this should take place in all aspects of our lives, not only when the boiler needs fixing. There are situations when it might be advisable to hire an expert or replace the item; don't be so committed to repair that you risk your own safety and wellbeing.

THE BENEFITS OF FINDING OUR OWN SOLUTIONS

Think of a car junkyard. These are places where we can find a part in perfect working condition for a very low price compared to buying new from a manufacturer. Yes, it takes time and effort to find a decent repair shop, to source a spare part or to sew up the hole in your old pair of socks when we could just buy a fresh pair, but there is much we can learn from taking time to mend our belongings. Fixing things and sourcing new parts can help us to gain a sense of accomplishment and contentment, allowing us to love and appreciate the items that we already possess. It's not difficult to sew on a missing button or repair a ripped seam, and if sewing isn't your thing, then friends and family may be able to help you. You could barter your time, for example cleaning their car, gardening or fixing their bike in exchange for some help with mending.

We learn more about how things work, and in the process can spend time bonding with children or family members, trying to find a solution together. While we labour, we could think about how our predecessors may have carried out similar tasks in the past, and how we can pass the skills on to others. Children today are often focused on screens and have little practical experience. Gardening and DIY are two activities that encourage children to connect with their surroundings and the world around them – and if you want to build a bridge between the virtual realm and the real one, ask them to find you online tutorials for repairing things. There's a world of information out there, and it's an excellent way of using the Internet to redirect them back into the practical world.

A switch in mindset about fixing things rather than throwing them away means that we can preserve heirloom items, maintaining them to be kept through the generations.

Paint
&
Paper

There is something deeply satisfying about standing back and admiring the results of our own DIY. Looking around, many of us can see examples of the work we have contributed to make our house a home. The shelves built in the kitchen, the painted the ceiling in the living area, the wonky tiles in the bathroom: not perfect, but our own work; something we contributed to and are proud of.

MAKING YOUR HOME YOUR OWN

DIY is important; we need to take a break from technology and get the creative juices flowing. There are frequent opportunities to do this, from the minute we move in and the flat-pack needs assembling to redecorating and adding to our home over the years. Doing these tasks is an opportunity to see how we can be more mindful when faced with challenges.

A manual task can give us a great deal of satisfaction. Taking care of your garden, or finally painting that wall the colour you want makes you feel accomplished and brings happiness. Carpentry, likewise, is a good example of working with natural materials and making your own solution. If you have nowhere to store books, you could try building your own shelving. The sensory experience of buying the wood, measuring your space and making it how you want. The end result is not particularly important, as long as it isn't going to collapse; even if it's a bit rough, seeing the fruits of your labour will add to the uniqueness of your home and make it yours.

The benefits to the mind of painting a wall are clear to see. The end results look pristine and fresh, and fill us with satisfaction every time we stop to look at our handiwork. The repetitive nature of brush or roller strokes up and down the wall is meditative in its own way. We are forced to pay attention if we want an even wall coverage; care needs to be taken to avoid dripping the paint everywhere and we need to set aside everything else or we'll find the brush dried up when we return from whatever distracted us. Leaving the phone or doorbell to ring, we dedicate this time to getting the job done.

FINDING THE FLOW STATE

DIY projects are a chance to learn new skills. We often talk about 'flow state' when discussing mindfulness, and time spent in a flow can occur when you are focused on the task at hand. Writers and artists talk about flow state, but it can be also be achieved by something like wallpapering a room, becoming so focused on applying the paste and laying on the new paper neatly that everything else falls by the wayside. Upcycling an old piece of furniture is another way to get into flow: we can rescue something destined for landfill, which is good for the planet and feels like a positive thing to do, and then we settle into fixing it up. Yard sales and junk shops can be treasure troves for solid vintage furniture that requires a little skill to bring it back to life.

Sometimes it's the simple things, the quick and easy projects, that have the biggest impact in the home. A lick of paint on the scuffed skirting board, touching up the grouting on the kitchen tiles, making a shoe rack – little touches make a big difference to the overall ambience. Notice how you feel when deciding to embark on a new project; are you excited, or does it make your heart sink? Why is it that you react as you do? Do you ever feel in a flow state, when you are so immersed in something that you don't even notice time passing?

Getting into a manual activity is starting from nothing, progressing little by little and discovering new skills that we never knew we had. Provided we don't undertake too difficult a project for our first task, and provided we get the right teaching or support, we can quickly recognise our ability to learn pretty much anything we turn our minds to. This gives us a sense of pride and productivity. Carrying out an absorbing, productive task gives us mindful focus, gifting ourselves a break from the worries of our lives.

Colour

We may not spend much time thinking about how colour affects our moods, but when it comes to deciding on paint colours in our houses, it is a direct reflection of our personalities. When we enter our homes, colour is the first thing that strikes us. Do dark colours make you feel down and claustrophobic, or cosy and safe? Do light tones feel cold, or refreshing? There is no right or wrong with colour, or rules on how it affects us, so we should spend time thinking about what we like and whether we are happy with our current choice. We can exercise control over this; even in rental accommodation, we can source fabrics, bedding and cushions in shades that make us feel calm and comfortable.

THE JOY OF COLOUR

Looking at colour can give us the opportunity to be more mindful. When was the last time you sat down at home and really noticed the colours surrounding you? We see the wall colours, furniture, lighting and fabrics daily, but perhaps fail to actually notice their effect on us. The joy we get from a brightly coloured batik throw, taking us back to a holiday where we purchased it. The warmth we feel from snuggling under a clean, white, fluffy blanket when it's cold. These are our touchstones.

Colour affects people in many different ways, depending on where they live, the climate and light that surrounds them. As with all trends, colour variations come and go, this is why it is important to choose colour personal to us. We try to make our homes beautiful with colours that reflect our preferences and personalities, which is important, but the key is to discover tones that we truly love, as opposed to those we think we're supposed to like. How do we blend the colours into a pleasing combination? Or conversely, are we happiest with loud, clashing palettes? Perhaps our favourite combinations are the ones that invite a little bit of creativity and randomness into the home? It's up to you. Pay attention to how you feel, and it'll guide you to the right mixture.

FINDING THE IDEAL SCHEME

We naturally associate colours with emotions; when we are sad, we feel blue; when we are angry, we see red; when we're jealous, we meet the green-eyed monster. It is no great surprise to learn that colour can influence our moods just as it expresses our feelings.

When decorating a minimalist interior, it's all about creating a clean base. This is a good starting point and can allow you to see a space without embellishment and from there decide where to add the colour. Clean white walls can open up a space, while soft, nature-toned pieces in beiges and green can be more soothing to the eye. Perhaps by sticking to a neutral minimalist palette we can take inspiration from nature and with the addition of lots of green plants, bring the outside in.

Alternatively, you could throw away the interiors rule book and work out what sits right with you. When choosing your paint, get some samples, put them on the walls, sit with the colours you like, and turn your attention inwards. Try to write down a few words that come up when contemplating how colour affects your mood in the home.

Perhaps there isn't enough comfort gained from the colours around you, and you're not in the position to take on any major redecoration. This doesn't mean you're debarred from a mindfulness-friendly space, though: you don't need to overhaul everything to adjust your surroundings. The simple act of placing some vibrant flowers on the table or filling a fruit bowl with vivid lemons and limes can perk up a space from the minute you walk into it. Moving a luscious red lamp from the bedroom into the lounge could be just the thing you need to both calm the bedroom and lift the energy. There is no rulebook you have to follow, simply the way that you react when you see it. Take that time to stop and reflect; you may be amazed at how a few quick changes can affect the whole home and the way you feel within it.

Stop to
Smell the Roses

Smell is the sense that can connect us most vividly with our past. The aroma of a favourite meal as it comes out of the oven, the scent of fresh laundry on your clothes, sand and sun cream mixed together on a sunny day . . . these can go right to our souls. We can see this clearly with children, who don't hide their feelings and react strongly when they smell manure on the fields or a food that they don't like: deep down, though we may be too polite to say so, we are passionate about what hits our noses. And while most of us like flowers but dislike rotting fish, how we respond to smells remains unique to each individual; the memories they trigger are unique to each of us. I remember the scent of my mother's perfume, the Christmas ham cooking on the stove, the smell of bonfires on our clothes on a Sunday afternoon. These take me straight back to childhood and remind me of carefree days.

By introducing certain smells into the home, we can trigger our own unique memories; in turn, we are introducing these scents to visitors and others in the household. Our sense of smell is linked to our limbic system, nerves in the brain connected with strong emotions and recall: our reaction to smell is more heartfelt than to any other sense.

A TRIGGER FOR THE SENSES

Close your eyes for a moment and breathe in through your nose. What aromas can you pick out? Try to name each one as you become more aware of them. Are they pleasant or not? Do they trigger sensations in your body? The smell of bacon cooking can make my stomach rumble; the smell of freshly cut grass brings a spring to my step and an urge to head outdoors.

We begin the day with smell, perhaps the scent of the soap we wash with, maybe pouring out the first cup of coffee in the kitchen as we begin our familiar morning ritual. Coffee is a good example of inviting smell into the home each day: when we open a bag of fresh beans and inhale the aroma, this is an opportunity to practise mindful breathing. For one minute, we can breathe in for seven, hold for four and out for seven, and repeat a couple of times. This brings us into the present and makes us feel calmer. The whiff of coffee in the kitchen is connected with an act of self-care: we are taking time out of our day to look after ourselves and spend a few moments over a drink we enjoy.

SMALL BUT POWERFUL CHANGE

Fresh flowers evoke all sorts of emotions and make the house smell wonderful. Which rooms do you want to relax in? Would it be nice to wake up to the scent of flowers by your bedside, or would a few vases dotted around the home work better? The act of choosing the flowers can be a mindful experience; look at the shapes and textures of the leaves, the relaxing or stimulating colours of the petals, and the scent you might bring home – perhaps the powerful perfume of a lily, or the gentle aroma of a freesia. Fresh flowers are a treat, but you could have a bunch of dried herbs such as rosemary and thyme on hand to sniff as an everyday pick-me-up. Similarly, flowers are often used in essential oils; lavender to evoke calm and relaxation is a popular choice, and once of the safer oils to use near bare skin. A few drops on the pillow at night or in a bathtub can be a useful element of your bedtime routine.

Cooking, meanwhile, offers an opportunity to explore our sense of smell, and by doing so, create a powerful visceral connection to what we're doing. For example, the process of making a casserole can be mindful if we can stop and notice the aroma, how it makes us feel, the sense of anticipation and comfort, and we consider what would make it taste even better, like adding more herbs or a splash of wine. It is worth taking our time in the act of cooking – after all, we are creating smells that may one day trigger memories for our families and friends.

Slow Down
with Green

Numerous studies have shown that proximity to a plant can make humans healthier and less stressed, promoting general wellbeing and happiness. There's even a treatment for mental illness known as horticultural therapy; plants pick us up when we're low.

PLANTS FOR WELLBEING

Having a living thing to care for gives us responsibility. If we don't water it, prune it or expose it to light, then it may die. Taking care of the plant and appreciating how it is growing is mindful in itself: the process of looking after your plants can bring you straight into the present. Focus on the leaves, study the stems and veins and watch how they spread across the plant. Spray the plant, wipe down the leaves, nurture it, love it. The plant will be stronger, and the process will create a quiet, positive space in which to de-stress.

Looking after plants is not as straightforward as it may seem; I speak from experience. It takes time to know whether to water too much or too little, whether it will wilt or flourish near a heat source, and what level of light will suit it best. It's a skill that will be expressed in life itself: seeing a plant you've tended put out new leaves is a message from another living thing that you've paid attention. Spending a little time on plants can go a long way for wellbeing in the home.

OUTDOOR PLANTING

Even if you live in a city-centre apartment with a tiny balcony, you could plant tomatoes in the spring, herbs for year-round culinary use, or colourful flowers in pots to add interest to the space. If there is no outdoor space, you could use window boxes to grow and nurture plants and flowers. You can plant for the seasons, letting your flowers and herbs show you how time goes on.

Whatever your planting space, different seasons call for different kinds of cultivation, so it's a call to be in touch with the changes in weather and daylight. Each week you can plan a set time to take care of your plants, being alert to their changing needs. While you're about it, if you have an outdoor space, you can incorporate planting that welcomes wildlife, connecting you even more with nature. The best herb varieties to encourage bees and butterflies are lavender, mint, rosemary, thyme and sage; all hardy plants, low maintenance and easy to keep, whether in pots or in the ground.

A REFUGE FOR THE MIND

Creating an indoor garden is not a major undertaking, but the addition of attractive houseplants can bring a new source of pleasure into the home. Over time, you can see the changes as your plants grow and develop new leaves and blooms. You could even propagate new shoots and give the baby plants to friends and family. (Although do bear in mind that certain plants are poisonous to humans or animals, and keep them well out of reach if this might be the case. Plants, like every other living thing, need to be treated with respect.)

When you feel like things are getting on top of you in life, nurturing plants can help you get back in control. While you will never be able to fully have your life in order, you can decide how to arrange your plants, what vegetables you want to grow, where the pot plants can move to, and how frequently you feed and water them. Bad day at work? Spend some time looking after your indoor plants, wiping off the dust and checking they are not too dry. Outside, cut back the deadheads, turn over the soil and pull up the weeds, leaving a clean canvas for your other plants to thrive. The act of caretaking is healing in itself: by handling your plants with gentleness and skill, care and attention, you are literally growing yourself a better living environment. You do it for them and for you at the same time, experiencing a balance between being the one who cares and the one who is cared for. Look after your botanical friends, and let them cheer you up.

Minimalist Living

If most of us were asked what we would take to a desert island, we might say music, books, photos or nice food. There are few references to the old sweaters in the back of the wardrobe, or the dreaded sock drawer full of odd socks. When it comes down to it, there really isn't much that is irreplaceable in a house. So, why do we hold on to so much stuff? This is not about stripping back your belongings to a bare minimum, but keeping things that bring a positive association, things that we want or need. A bibliophile may have shelves full of books, each one may trigger a memory and they may look like art itself, but do we need to keep them all? Could we give some to a friend?

BREAKING ATTACHMENTS

Why do we become so attached? Buddhism talks about non-attachment in many areas, for both people and things. This does not mean that we need to live alone with no belongings, but rather that in order to reach some kind of nirvana (your natural state) you cannot progress until you recognize that you are attached to stuff.

Some people get very attached to money, power or objects. The problem is that these are not permanent. Money can be lost, power can be taken away and objects can be stolen or destroyed. It is impossible to be truly satisfied with external things; we end up simply wanting more. So how can we work on being less attached to items in the home? When we think about the Buddhist idea that our actions are our only true belongings, then it makes things fairly simple when it comes to keeping the things we need or love.

In terms of our personal belongings, we know that eventually most things will wear out or break down.

Suppose, for instance, a fire destroyed our house and its contents: the more we placed our happiness in our personal items, the worse we'd suffer. We need instead to appreciate the things that we own, enjoy them, but try to remain a little detached. If we do this, then we allow ourselves the space to leave what we don't love, keep the things that we do and free up space for more valuable things in life.

LETTING GO

Sorting through our items can be exhausting. Each individual item, from a box of safety pins in a drawer to old letters from a relative, requires a decision about whether we keep it or let it go, sell it or donate it. When I have done this in the past, there are some items that I find easy to make a decision about and others that move from pile to pile without a final decision being made. For example, I had a piece of artwork on the wall, bought on holiday with the family, which I didn't actually like, but felt attached to because it triggered a memory of the trip we made. This should have been a simple decision because I didn't like the image, but it evoked happy memories that I held onto. In the end I donated the artwork to charity and put a photo up of the holiday as a replacement, but I could have used the space to add a different memory or simply left it as a blank area allowing space to think.

There are times in life when we change our identity. Perhaps we become a parent or get married and move in with another person, or we lose a parent or change neighbourhoods. These times make us address our belongings and look at how many we have and what no longer serves us; we can try to let some things go. Clearing out some of our things can feel a little like letting go of part of ourselves. This can be a painful sensation, and mindfulness is a good way to ride that discomfort out. We are in the world and of the world, every moment; with or without a particular possession, we are still who we are. If you can manage it, the feeling when we reduce these possessions is so freeing. You end up with less distraction in the home, more control of our belongings and a feeling of lightness that well repays the initial effort.

If you are struggling to let go of things, try asking yourself why you are really hanging onto them. What does an item mean to you and what memories have you attached to it? When you connect yourself to these emotions you will realize that those memories are always with you, they don't need to be triggered by an item. Maybe, give thanks to an item for triggering those memories and then, unless you love it, release it with a smile.

Animals
in the
Home

Dog owners often describe the glorious feeling that they experience when they arrive home to a warm welcome from their dogs. The excitement of hearing their owner turning the key in the lock can bring dogs bounding across the room, eager for a cuddle and stroke (perhaps they know that it's dinnertime). That unconditional love shown by animals can bring us right into the moment.

Our pets don't judge us. No matter how their day was, they are generally excited to see us walk through the door. We need not worry about our appearance or what mood we are in: if we're happy, they're happy; if we're sad, they are there for a snuggle. We often worry about how our mood will affect others, worry about judgement, or how we are perceived by others. These worries vanish when it comes to animals.

PROVIDING SUPPORT

Animals of many kinds can help provide social support, which is important to help us raise the feel-good chemicals in our brains, such as serotonin and dopamine. Hospitals and care homes use therapy animals such as dogs and cats for this very reason. Stroking pets can help to release anxiety, and even watching fish swim around their tank can help ease tension, which is why they are often found in hospitals and dentists waiting areas. The gentle rise and fall of a sleeping cat's belly can be relaxing and calming, helping us to tune into the moment and slow down our own breathing. All in all, pets create a lovely soothing moment for us to be present in.

LESS LOVABLE CREATURES

Not all animal experiences are as pleasant as snuggling down with a cat. There are times when we have unwanted guests in our homes, and this can be testing. Many otherwise brave people, even animal lovers, would admit to having one or two creepy-crawlies that they just don't like. An example would be spiders; many people have a deep fear of them that's quite immune to any suggestion that the spiders won't actually hurt them. Or we may have a fly infestation, testing our patience when trying to keep the house and our food clean, irritated by the endless buzzing. It can be all too easy to reach for a fly swatter or some wasp spray.

This, however, is not the most mindful approach. Chemicals sprays aren't great for the environment, and more generally, we share the planet with these amazing creatures and even the less desirable ones have a right to be here too.

Buddhists are animal lovers who try not to harm animals wherever possible. They believe that a soul may be reborn either in a human being or the body of an animal, both with a Buddha nature, and both with the possibility of becoming enlightened. This is what Buddhists avoid killing animals at all costs, even those pesky mosquitoes that bite.

You may not quite believe in human-souled wasps, but there is a lesson there: life is precious. If you're suffering from a phobia, try to sit with it mindfully. Don't judge yourself for being afraid; just let the fear happen, observe it, and don't overreact. As children, we are often full of curiosity for bugs and beasts of all shapes and sizes; see if you can observe as a child would, as openly as possible. Even the creepiest of creatures is extraordinary if you can view it through mindful eyes.

LEARNING FROM ANIMALS

Animals can teach us so much about the way we are, and we don't need a pet to do this. We can watch them playing, and observe how they appear to be completely in the moment. A dog chewing on his bone, or a bird outside the window patiently building his nest, twig after twig. This can be a wonderful meditative experience to observe.

These living creatures give us the opportunity to embrace our silliness. It is hard not to smile when watching animals, and this can be really helpful for snapping us out of our trickier states of mind. We can practise mindfulness by simply tuning into our senses in the present moment, by paying attention to the touch of their fur or listening to the sounds that they make.

Time
for
Nothing

The idea of sitting and doing nothing can be so alien to us, it makes many feel uncomfortable. We have become a generation of multi-taskers, priding ourselves on our juggling skills. This may be useful up to a point, but there needs to be space in the home where nothing time can take place; this is how we guard ourselves against burnout.

Your environment affects the amount of nothing time you can take on, so have a look around your home to see if you can make it a friendlier space for that. For instance: can you prevent work devices from homing in on your attention? If you add an alarm clock to your bedroom, you needn't keep a phone by your bed to wake you up; if you put a clock on your kitchen wall, you don't need to check the time on your tablet. Add a soft couch, a comfy armchair, a few cushions or just a blanket. Anchor furniture around a window or fireplace rather than a TV, a space that looks welcoming to sit and just be.

SETTING BOUNDARIES

We frequently end up bringing work home with us, which is a sure way to inject stress into the home and affect our moods and relationships. Your job may require some from-home time, of course, but it doesn't have to take over the whole house: you can give it a designated space and keep it there, along with all your work-related items. If there isn't a desk, try a bag, folder or drawer where you can pack away papers and to-do lists, and then switch off your work emails until the following day.

Life admin also takes over at home. There is always something to be done; notes on the fridge, shopping lists on the backs of old envelopes, calendars on the wall and insurance documents to be renewed. These never-ending jobs can leave us feeling unable to relax. Designating time and space for this will allow you to focus on the tasks in hand and then put the items away, in order to free up both surface and mind space. One noticeboard, in an area away from our relaxing spaces, should be all you need to keep a record of the urgent things, the rest can be neatly filed away.

As well as choosing not to look at work notifications, there are other things you can do to switch off and become more present at home. It's completely natural to talk about your day over dinner, but check how much discussing work brings you down or makes you stressed. If you had a stressful day, you don't necessarily want to bring the negative energy home; put a limit on your work chat. Try not to feel guilty; you will work better for the break.

SLOWING DOWN, SWITCHING OFF

Success is often judged by how busy people seem: the more hectic their lives, the more important we assume they are. Imagine if instead, we measured success by our space and time to do nothing. We would plan our lives quite differently, living our lives slowly rather than fast, wanting less rather than more. We can make a personal choice to measure our own success, however, by managing the juggle to create quiet moments. When turning down invitations, if people ask if we are busy, we can say we are busy doing nothing; if you make it clear that you're not snubbing friends, just in need of some rest, your honesty may get a better reaction than you expect.

Mindfulness is a powerful thing when practised regularly; it can help you to de-stress in the middle of work as well as switch off after work. Try to begin your nothing time on the way back from work or your day out: meditate with some ambient instrumental music or a mindfulness app to get you into the right frame of mind when you arrive home. If there is no commute, then aim to do something each evening to signal the end of the working day; a ten-minute meditation is perfect for many people. Everyone feels like they couldn't possibly fit any more into their day, but the truth is that even a few minutes is worth it, and once you start enjoying the quiet, you'll find yourself more eager to make time.

Urges & Necessities

Wanting more can be a real challenge for most of us. Sitting at home, it can be easy to crave, whether for something immediate like a bar of chocolate from the shop, a takeaway meal instead of the hassle of cooking, or a friend to come over and cheer us up, or something more drastic like a bigger house. Out of all of our emotions and experiences, the desire for more is the most prevalent – but often when we get what we want, our desires are briefly satisfied, and then a new urge is formed.

RESISTING THOSE URGES

Surfing our urges is a technique developed by the late Alan Marlatt, a notable psychologist who coined the theory to help us resist our desires. We can think of an urge as an impulse to engage in an old habit, such as getting home and opening a bottle of wine every night, or online shopping from the comfort of the sofa without thinking about what you already have in your wardrobe. With urge surfing, we observe the physical feeling like a wave as it rises and falls and continue to do this until it passes. This normally lasts no more than thirty minutes, and helps us to deepen our practice of mindfulness in the home, perhaps it saves us money at the same time.

As you're sitting at home, you might notice a desire to book a spontaneous holiday, or to order in some junk food. If you turn your awareness inwards, becoming more mindful and noticing the way that the desires flow and surge in and out of your brain, you can begin to note how the wanting wanes as you simply hang out with your sudden needs. As you listen to them become less and less urgent as time goes on, you can begin to see that the desire passes. Just like everything else, it is impermanent. That moment of going from being aware of the desire to seeing it pass out of range can feel freeing. When you realize that you don't have to act on every desire that enters your mind, you realize that you're not a slave to your own whims. We can switch from wanting to not wanting something, making us feel content with what we have already. The key here is to practise with this meditation tool as soon as one of these urges surfaces, so that you can begin to use it with ease when faced with our next challenge of desire.

DON'T DO, JUST BE

It can be easy to think that we don't have time to meditate. When it comes to managing desires, though, it's important to practice when you don't particularly want anything as well as when you do; you can think of the last time you wanted something, didn't get it,

and were fine afterwards. In this way, you can build up
your psychological muscles so that next time you find
yourself craving something you'd be wiser to do
without, you'll be prepared. The cliché 'Don't do, just be'
is very relevant: when meditation is a habit, it can help
us to divert our thoughts and actions down a positive
path without even thinking.

NOTHING LASTS FOREVER

These emotions that overtake us so frequently are
impermanent, and it is important to remember this.
We know this intellectually, but somehow we haven't
internalized it – or at least, when faced with our desires,
it's easy to forget. I find myself at home criticizing
myself for things that I have said and done that I could
have done differently, and then I put this discomfort
onto annoyances in the home. I notice the chipped
paint on the bathroom wall, the door that creaks; this
makes me want a new door, a tidier home, a bigger
space: my discomfort turns into desire for solutions.

The solution should be trying to observe my thoughts, and then let them go. It isn't really the door or the size of the rooms that's bothering me: it's my thoughts, and those, I can manage for myself. What I actually need to do is move on and realize that even if I got the bigger home, the door wasn't creaky, and everything was immaculate, I would find something new to criticize and want more anyway. Surfing the urges gets easier with time, allowing us to focus on things other than fulfilling our transitory desires.

Embrace
the
Imperfect

When we find ourselves disappointed, we could consider shifting perspective to embrace the uniqueness of life with all of its beauty, completely unique to every individual. At home, we are normally at our most relaxed, and this makes it a good place reflect on our lives and evaluate the good and the bad.

It's harder to do this when we're critical about our homes. Mindfulness can really help to embrace the imperfect – as long as we don't try to be perfect in the way we go about it. We tell ourselves that we should be doing more meditation, just as we should be exercising more, should go to the party even if we really don't want to. Whatever our goal is, using the word 'should' is never a wise idea. The good news is that it's also an easy word to stop using.

YOUR LIFE IS UNIQUE

Striving for perfection is not the aim of mediation. If everything were perfect, would life be any fun? If things came easily to us, there would be no challenges and we would be lost. How do we stop being so critical of ourselves and our lives, and try to stop unrealistic expectations? The first step in changing anything is awareness, and with meditation, we can pay attention to the moments when we criticize ourselves and ask whether this way of thinking is serving us well.

There are many things in the home that we can try to see a little differently. The never-ending washing-up, mopping away muddy footprints, the laundry, cleaning the bathroom: it can be simple to see those jobs as a result of mess and disarray. If we look at things differently and know that we cannot be doing all of those tasks at once, then we can see them for what they are; things that need to be done in an allocated time. The sofa may have marks on it, but there is no way we can afford a new sofa at present – we can either cover it with a throw, or remember the joy of the chocolate ice cream that made the mark. Imperfections are the traces life leaves behind, and we can enjoy them as they bear witness to an ever-changing existence.

TAKE LIFE AS IT COMES

We strive for perfection in life when there is no need. Take meditation itself. Often, we are too harsh on ourselves for not being able to clear our minds, for thinking too much during mindful practices. This exhausting self-judgement defeats the purpose; we are simply trying to aim for the ability to be more present. For example, sitting down to do a guided meditation might make you feel irritated, leading to internal chatter: 'I should be able to do this! Why am I no good at meditating?' In the home, perhaps looking out of the window and watching the sun set is enough to make you feel truly present each day; this in itself is a type of meditation.

When we talk about being in the present and being mindful, people often get confused between the two. Being in the present is an essential component of being mindful, but it's not the whole picture; being mindful is something a little bit broader. When we look at a pet for example, a furry kitten bouncing around the house playing with a ball of string, at first glance they seem completely in the moment, very much involved in the world of scent and play and simply being, but to call them mindful would be a stretch too far. They are just caught up in the present and the momentary experience, but without the added dimension of any self-reflection.

Mindfulness involves letting go of expectations – that is, of an attachment to the result turning out a certain way. If we surrender to the idea that we can't and needn't control everything, our expectation is significantly reduced, leading to less disappointment if things don't work out as we had hoped. We can remove ourselves from the outcome, and therefore become more resilient if things don't turn out the way we wanted them to. By shifting our focus from trying to make sure everything goes as planned to accepting our feelings as they come and go, we create a place of safety within ourselves that can survive setbacks.

Letting
the
Light In

When we are lucky enough to have clear skies, sun streaming through our windows and light in our rooms, we're given an instant mood lift. In Buddhist ceremonies, you can usually see a candle or lamp, symbolizing that we

should put others in front of ourselves and think of them first, removing our egos where possible. The Buddha regarded the 'light' of wisdom as the most important light of all: his eyes are closed so that the mind can be understood internally, in particular how the mind can regenerate and free itself from suffering.

Taking that into account, we can look at both how we can bring light into the home, and the importance of looking within for our energy and joy. Humans were made to be outside, so letting more natural brightness into your home can help attune your body to nature – although it doesn't need to have a natural light source in order for you to have good lighting; there are many things you can do to create well-lit areas.

ADAPT THE LIGHTING TO THE SPACE

The brightness or darkness of a room changes its mood, just as it does its perceived size. Natural and artifical lighting help with the feeling of space in a home, while dark rooms feel significantly smaller than they often are. Similarly, light can feel as though it's being absorbed by large, bulky or close-packed furniture. You can counter this with corner and wall lamps, which really brighten a space when natural light is not available. Skylights or large windows are the best way of attracting more daylight, but if you don't have these, keep the space feeling bright and fresh with voile panels or thin cotton curtains, maintaining privacy but letting the brightness in. In the bedroom, you could add a blackout blind behind the curtains or voiles to keep out the early morning sun.

Using a yellow light in the bedroom at night-time will help you relax, but the detrimental effects of the blue light emitted by phone and computer screens have been well documented. The artificial light disrupts your body's production of melatonin, the hormone that regulates sleep. Natural light has the opposite effect; it helps you to be more energetic by day and sleepy at night, realigning your circadian rhythm with the rising and setting of the sun. Whenever possible, allow the natural sky to illuminate your home; if it's quite dark, try reading a book next to the window. By not turning on a light you are saving yourself money and not requiring fossil fuels to be burned to generate electricity.

BRIGHTENING YOUR DAY

Opening your home to more natural sunlight has many benefits to your health and to the planet; it can make you warmer, more comfortable and happier. But light is as much about the inside as the outside of our minds: there's a reason why we talk about 'brightening your day'. We can use various methods to have more peaceful and positive experiences. When you find yourself going through the auto-pilot mechanics of your daily routine, take five minutes to think about initiating positive emotions. This will more than likely help to add some sparkle to the day ahead, whatever it may bring.

By shining a light on our internal emotional landscape, we can pick up where we are feeling stressed and where we need space. Part of reaching a better balance is to recognize where our limits are. This is a conscious choice based on an understanding of what is healthy for us right now – not going into our emotions repeatedly and ruminating but simply recognising them as they arise. This helps us to develop some emotional agility and bring some illumination into our daily lives. Combine this with opening the blinds and the curtains, and we will have a significant chance of more calm in the home.

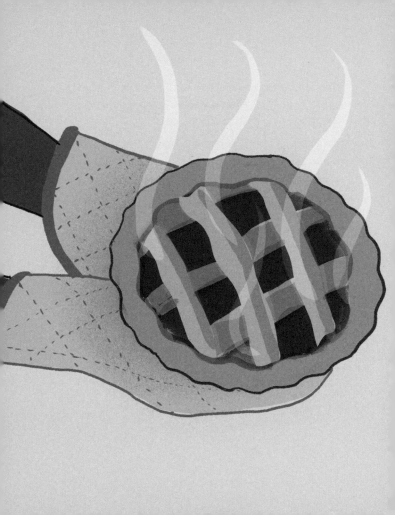

Creativity
at Home

When we are creative, we feel alive and fulfilled. Our home space offers many opportunities in the home to be creative, and personalizing it with our own ideas and handiwork allows us to feel more deeply embraced when we settle down there. From knitting a blanket to snuggle under in the winter, to arranging a gallery wall of our favourite art and images, there are plenty of ways in which we can mindfully curate and create our environment.

As I grew up, my granny would mend all the holes in my clothes, make curtains for my bedroom and knit while listening to the radio. She spent hours making and rolling out pastry, creating delights in the kitchen for us all to enjoy. There is something deeply satisfying looking around the home and seeing the wonders of your work, no matter how big or small they are. These small wonders are reflections of ourselves, and often trigger happy memories. They encourage us to be present in our homes, to look at what we have contributed to our space and enjoy the work we have done.

EXPLORING NEW IDEAS

When discussing the benefits of mindfulness, people often focus on stress management; after all, few things help one deal better with the stresses of everyday life than regular meditation practice. But meditation also quietens the over-active mind – and the more clutter-free your mind is, the more space it has for new and better ideas. It supports the free flow of our thoughts without immediate evaluation, and should help people to generate ideas. The main barrier to our creativity is ourselves; our minds editing ideas and rejecting off-the-wall possibilities before exploring them fully to see whether they have any merit.

Just because we don't know how to do something doesn't mean that we cannot learn it, no matter what our age may be. When we think about creativity, we often think of making things, and of course that's part of it, but the real essence is growing and learning. The Internet, for instance, can be a useful tool for teaching ourselves new skills or finding the answers to queries we may have about what materials we need for a project. There are online tutorials for curtain making, macramé wall hangings, training yourself to draw, learning a new language: if it's an activity people do, there will be people showing you how to do it on the Internet. All of these things can inspire and encourage us to have a little space for ourselves, while teaching us to be more mindful at the same time.

Learning new things also helps us engage further with people in our community. We can join an evening class or workshop if we want to make something for the home, or ask locally if someone can help to teach us a new skill. Skill swapping is becoming more common, such as artists offering to teach a painting tutorial in exchange for a box of vegetables from someone's allotment. Both parties are fulfilled, and it is mutually beneficial. We can enjoy looking at the end result in our homes, reminding us of happy, creative times.

ENJOYING THE PROCESS

While being creative, our brains are active but peaceful, whether we're colouring, baking, writing or crafting. You are using both your creative self and your analytical self, and as you fully engage your mind, you are acting without agenda; it happens without noticing it. Sometimes the things that we make without over-thinking are the ones that we are most proud of and that others seem to appreciate more. Maybe this is because we enter a meditative state whereby we can shut off our inner critic, and just allow ourselves to be. This present moment awareness can help us overcome difficult thoughts, keeping us balanced and attuned with the positive, vital and happy aspects of ourselves. Making and displaying the objects that we create in this mindset can lead to feelings of satisfaction and accomplishment every time we pass by them; a regular reminder of the meditative moments we spent making them with such care.

Projects don't always turn out as we want them to. This should not put us off; looking mindfully at being creative in the home means trying not to be perfect. As children we would paint and colour, print and bake, not striving for perfection but having fun. When choosing an activity, remember to enjoy the process, whatever the outcome.

Each Night
We Sleep

On average, we spend a third of our lives sleeping, and no less than food and drink, sleep is vital for maintaining good mental and physical health. The trouble is that rest doesn't always come: our busy brains

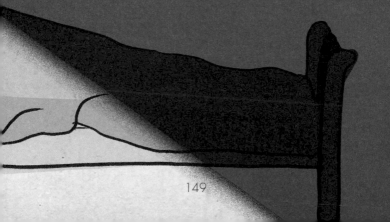

buzz with thoughts, and just to make it worse, we start to worry that tomorrow will be ruined by tiredness, and get irritated that we can't control our sleep. Who can feel calm at home when that's happening? If this sounds like a familiar problem, the first step is to make your surroundings as conducive to rest as possible.

A RESTFUL ENVIRONMENT

We all need a restful night, and the key to achieving this is our environment. From the colours of the walls to the lighting by our bedside, the removal of digital devices and keeping clutter to a minimum, our sleeping space needs to be well thought out and as soothing as possible.

We can create an environment that reduces stress, so that if we do find ourselves awake in the night, we are in a calm place and can relax in it. Most of us will have a bit of clutter around the bedroom, books on the bedside table or clothes on the chair, but too much mess is never going to be relaxing when we are trying to get to sleep. Sneaky under-bed storage and cupboards can really help when it comes to hiding things away.

USING MEDITATION TO PREPARE FOR SLEEP

Try a meditation to wind down at the very end of the day, and see if it improves your quality of sleep. A good meditation can help to let go of all the day's thoughts and worries, to relax the body with deep breaths, and in turn, relax the mind. You can use the practice while tucked up in bed, or perhaps sitting on a rug next to it, to bring a sense of resolution to the day's activities and practise feeling gratitude for what you have in your daily life.

A good way to start is by imagining one or two things from your day that you are grateful for, and possibly take for granted normally. They can be very small, like the warm feeling of a jumper on an icy day, or might be larger and applicable to the wider world, but picture something that inspires a sincere appreciation of the day you're winding down from. As you hold the feelings that are inspired in your mind, notice how your body responds. Take that positivity and the feelings of contentment and gratitude, and shrink your awareness from the past to the present moment. Feel the weight of your body on the chair, floor or the bed, the warmth of the room and the restful atmosphere. Allow yourself to be grounded in that moment and let the feelings of happiness and gratitude flow through you. Bringing gratitude to the end of our day is the perfect mindful way to set yourself up for a restful night's sleep.

HELP YOURSELF TO SLEEP SOUNDLY

Maybe we cannot sleep because you're dealing with strong feelings. It may well be that you need to feel them, but since you can't do anything about them right now, a notepad by your bed is a good compromise: why not write them down and see if they're still just as worrisome in the morning? When we sleep, we breathe deeply, so it could help to increase the levels of oxygen: have some plants in the room or, if it's a warm night, you could let some fresh air in. Keep some fresh water within reach to stay hydrated.

Your bedroom is your sanctuary; look after it and keep it as one. When we can't drift off, no matter what we have done in preparation, we can remind ourselves that at some point we will sleep; our bodies need to. Reading a book, meditating or listening to relaxing music will take away the anxiety of not sleeping. If we tell ourselves that we can read all night, it will relax the body and mind, allowing sleep to come sooner.

Bring Beauty
into
Your Space

Many of us make our daily stress even greater by adding in a layer of self-judgement. We make mistakes, and then we are tough on ourselves; this usually only leads to more negative behaviour, as we don't operate at our best when crushed by our emotions. We can start to take control of this at home by practising mindfulness.

TIME TO REFLECT

What do you do in your free time at home? Do you turn on the television as soon as you walk through the door? Perhaps you head for a glass of wine or start cooking immediately. It's a natural impulse, but a more mindful approach is to come to terms with what's going on in our minds rather than escaping through means such as alcohol, television or other distractions. If we're really going to feel all right, we have to take time to accept and acknowledge our thoughts, emotions and physical feelings. When we know we can sit with the problems in our lives, we feel more free: thoughts we have practiced experiencing mindfully are a lot less frightening. At home, we can use our spare time to examine our feelings.

Within our homes, we have the opportunity to change what we don't like, just as we do with our minds. We know that our emotions are always in flux, and when we have uncomfortable feelings, they override us so much that, almost as if we are under a spell, it can seem as if they will never end. We do not think or see clearly when we are affected in this way. Mindfulness can help us with these emotions, but to get the benefits, we need to make time to practise at home.

FACING OUR EMOTIONS

Our homes are always changing. The light within waxes and wanes depending on the weather outside; the amount of mess depends on how busy we are at work and what other commitments we have. When it is raining outside, we don't panic that it will rain forever, or that our house will always be dark inside: we know that it will end eventually. At some point, the rain will stop, our houses will become brighter and we won't be as busy at work. These issues won't be permanent, and neither will our emotions.

Emotions are there for a reason, and we need to listen to them. If we can hear them without trying to suppress or distract ourselves from them, they offer information about what is actually important and what we need to do within ourselves, in relation to our environment or with other people. We may arrive home, for instance, to see that our partner forgot to empty the bins and now the house smells; we react with anger. Take a step back. We know that it can be easy to forget to put the bins out, so by stopping and examining our immediate reaction we may realize we have brought home external factors from a bad day at work and taken these out on our partner. We can use our home to take responsibility for our inner feelings, identifying the good and bad habits within ourselves.

INTERNAL HOME SPACE

Reflecting on our feelings enables us to start separating what sets us off and what is really at the root of our emotion. Often, it isn't the thing itself that's so bad: behind it is an unexpressed need trying to make itself felt. Everything in life wants to be acknowledged; once we do that, we find that a door opens to take away the intensity and we can allow positive change to happen.

Let's be realistic: even when you practise mindfulness regularly, you will still get stressed by the washing-up gathering in the sink, you still need to do the laundry, and will occasionally be late getting to work. Nothing much might change in your environment – and yet everything might change inside of you. The more you practise mindfulness, the easier it will be to ride out the inevitable troubles at home that life throws at you, and the richer and more vivid will be the happy moments that you cherish. Observe the transformation that takes place within; you may find that you can navigate life more skilfully, with more love and kindness, and choose to see things in a more positive light.

ACKNOWLEDGEMENTS

Thank you to my husband Dan, who practises meditation every day and reminds me to slow down when things are busy. My three boys, Jack, Cody and Sam, inspire me to be more present, and in return, I aim to set them up with a good mindful toolkit for the future. My sister, Sarah, who read through many of the chapters before I submitted them and is my daily sunshine. And my friends Treg and Sig, for their encouragement always.